THE BEST OF
INDIA

THE BEST OF
INDIA
A COOKBOOK

Balraj Khanna

Food Photography by Steven Mark Needham

CollinsPublishersSanFrancisco
A Division of HarperCollinsPublishers

First published in USA 1993 by CollinsPublishersSanFrancisco
1160 Battery Street, San Francisco, CA 94111

Produced by Smallwood and Stewart Inc.,
New York City

© 1993 Smallwood and Stewart, Inc.

Food Editor: Yvonne McFarlane
Editor: Judith Blahnik
Food Styling: Anne Disrude
Prop Styling: Bette Blau

Photography credits: Jeffrey Alford/Asia Access:
1; 2-3; 7; 21; 29; 51; 77; 84; 87
Prop credits: Annapurna Restaurant, p. 11, plate; p. 14, copper bowls;
p. 25, "vessel"; p. 43, chalice & covered basket; p. 49, fabric & stone dish;
p. 53, platter & bowls; p. 59, copper cups, beads & fabric; p. 61, elephant;
p. 62, bowl; p. 71, bowl; p. 83 spoons & stone board; p. 88, plate,
cup & fabric. Casablanca Restaurant, p. 67, plate.

Library of Congress Cataloging-in-Publication Data

Balraj Khanna
    The Best of India/Balraj Khanna :
food photography by Steven Mark Needham
        p. cm.
    Includes index
    ISBN 0-00-255223-X
    1. Cookery, India.   I. Title
    TX724.5.I4k49   1993
    641.5954--dc20   93-8401
                                                CIP

Printed in China

Contents

Introduction

Indian food, like Indian culture, is among the most distinctive in the world. Its complexity is like India itself, a country of staggering contrasts and diversity ~ geographic, climatic, and social. In the North are the world's highest mountains, the perennially snow-clad Himalayas, and the evergreen Punjab, the granary of India. To the West burns the barren Thar desert, while in the East are the steamy swamps of the Gangetic Delta. There are tropical jungles, great rivers, a seemingly endless coastline, dust storms, sandstorms, and, not least, the truculent monsoon, upon which all life in India depends.

Socially, Hindus form the bulk of the population ~ about 85 percent of its nearly one billion people ~ though they live side by side with followers of most of the other leading world religions, all maintaining their own customs, beliefs, rituals, and taboos. Hindus don't eat beef, believing the cow to be sacred; Muslims (10 percent of the population) abhor pork, considering the pig unclean; Parsees happily eat both. Buddhists and Jains

Garlands for Hindu temple offerings

eat no meat of any sort, revering all forms of life. In the North, wheat is the staple grain, while in the South and in Bengal, it is rice. All Indians cook with the same spices, but the combinations vary from region to region, and every housewife has her own blend of spices, handed down by her mother.

Historically, Indian food, like Indian culture, has been profoundly influenced by foreigners, especially the magnificent Mughals, who conquered India in the sixteenth century and ruled it for three hundred years. Coming from Central Asia, the Mughals were particularly fascinated by all things Persian. They introduced many of the highly aromatic dishes that are popular at the Indian table today ~ delicate rice pullao; savory pastries stuffed with meat and vegetable fillings; spinach cooked with onion, ginger, and cardamom; cumin-spiced split peas; stewed chicken with almonds and raisins; and a variety of marinated meats braised in yogurt sauces.

The aim of this book is to introduce Indian dishes with authentic tastes and flavors. Most Indians are vegetarians for whom an average meal would consist of one or two seasonal vegetables, a dish of dal, rice, and freshly made bread to scoop up the food. A nonvegetarian family might eat one dish of fish, meat, or chicken, along with fresh bread such as chapatis, vegetables, and dal. Raitas and chutneys are the relishes that accompany every meal. There are no hors d'oeuvre as such, but at an elaborate wedding feast or formal banquet as many as twenty dishes may be presented at the same time.

A well-stocked Indian kitchen has nearly thirty fresh spices and other flavorings on the shelf. Certain ingredients ~ fresh chili, garlic, ginger, and onion ~ are used in most dishes, as are the basic spices ~ ground turmeric, coriander, cumin, and chili powder, as well as such secondary flavorings as cinnamon, cardamom, cloves, mustard seeds, poppy seeds, and asafetida.

Most cooks are deft at extracting a variety of flavors from a single spice, simply by roasting it, frying it in hot oil, or grinding it. And ingredients are often combined in adventurous ways ~ cumin with mint, for example or cinnamon with nutmeg, mace, and black pepper ~ producing a variety of tastes and textures in what would otherwise be very simple dishes.

These classic recipes are the best examples of the Indian genius with spices. Through them you will discover the rich and varied pleasures of this glorious cuisine.

Balraj Khanna

Aam Chatni

Fresh Mango Chutney

With more than one thousand varieties growing
throughout the country, the mango is truly the king of fruits in India.
Its sweet flesh makes wonderful fresh desserts and is often added to pilafs,
curry dishes, pickles, and chutneys. Hard, sour mangoes are sun-dried
and ground into powder that is used to add tang to many dishes. A slightly
unripe mango is used here to give a sweet-and-sour taste to this delicious
chutney, which should be eaten right away ~ it won't keep. Buy the mangoes
the day you intend to make the chutney, as they spoil rapidly.

*2 medium slightly unripe
mangoes, peeled, pitted &
coarsely chopped*

*1½ teaspoons finely chopped
fresh mint*

½ teaspoon sugar

½ teaspoon salt

Pinch of ground coriander

Pinch of ground cumin

Pinch of chili powder

Pinch of grated nutmeg

Pinch of ground cloves

*Pinch of freshly ground
black pepper*

In a food processor or blender, combine all the ingredients and process until slightly chunky.

Turn the chutney into a serving bowl. Cover and refrigerate 30 minutes before serving. Makes 1 cup.

Pudina Chatni

Mint Chutney *(picture p. 14)*

This chutney is a light, fresh dip with a cool, minty taste
and can be served with all kinds of dishes. It goes particularly well with
Pakoras (p. 20) or Samosas (p. 17). For a creamier mixture, add 2 tablespoons
plain yogurt or, for a sharper taste, add 1 tablespoon lemon or lime
juice. Pudina Chatni cannot be stored; eat it when it's fresh.

*⅓ cup coarsely chopped
    fresh mint*

⅓ cup coarsely chopped onion

*⅓ cup coarsely chopped
    fresh coriander*

*1 medium fresh hot green chili,
    seeded & coarsely chopped*

¼ cup cold water

1 teaspoon salt

In a food processor or blender, combine all the ingredients and process until smooth. Turn the chutney into a serving bowl. Cover and refrigerate until well chilled. Makes 1 cup.

Hare Dhaniya ki Chatni

Fresh Coriander Chutney

In many Indian households, this hot chutney is made
fresh every day and served at each meal. The tangy flavor perks up
Indian-style scrambled eggs at breakfast, provides a good foil for appetizers
at dinner, and is a popular complement to mild meat and rice dishes.
For a more fiery version, double the amount of hot chilies.

1 cup fresh coriander leaves

*1 medium fresh hot green chili,
   seeded & coarsely chopped*

*One ½-inch piece fresh ginger,
   peeled & coarsely chopped*

1 teaspoon ground cumin

2 tablespoons water

Salt

In a blender, combine the coriander, chili, ginger, cumin, and water, and process 5 to 10 seconds, or until the mixture is smooth and slightly moist; add a teaspoon more water if necessary. Add salt to taste. Turn the chutney into a serving bowl. Cover with plastic wrap and refrigerate until ready to serve. Makes 1 cup.

Kachoomber & Pudina Chatni, page 12

Kachoomber

This is a very popular salad, ideal for serving on hot days with grilled and barbecued dishes. To vary the recipe, try substituting finely sliced shallots for the onion or lime juice for the lemon, or add a teaspoon of Dijon-style mustard to the dressing. Make this salad just before serving it.

½ teaspoon cumin seeds

4 tablespoons olive oil

2 tablespoons red wine vinegar

1 tablespoon lemon juice

2 garlic cloves, minced

1 cup thinly sliced onion rings

4 medium ripe tomatoes, sliced

1 small cucumber, thinly sliced

Pinch of freshly ground black pepper

Salt

5 large fresh mint leaves, finely chopped

Heat a small skillet over medium-high heat. Add the cumin seeds and toast, stirring constantly, 20 to 30 seconds. Transfer to a plate and allow to cool. In a large salad bowl, whisk the oil, vinegar, and lemon juice until blended. Add the garlic, onion, tomatoes, cucumber, pepper, and salt to taste; toss well. Sprinkle with the cumin seeds and mint, toss again, and serve. Serves 4 to 6.

Kheere ka Raita

Cucumber and Mint Raita *(picture p. 39)*

A cool and refreshing relish, raita is always the perfect
partner for very hot and spicy dishes. Some cooks also like to serve it as an
accompaniment to mildly spiced foods, claiming it helps in digestion.
Traditionally, raita is made with a variety of ingredients and flavorings added to
the yogurt base. For a variation on this recipe, stir in 3 tablespoons
freshly grated apple just before serving. Raita does not keep well, so it should
be prepared no more than 30 minutes before serving.

2 cups plain yogurt

*1 medium cucumber, peeled,
seeded & finely diced*

½ teaspoon salt

*⅛ teaspoon freshly ground
black pepper*

*2 tablespoons finely chopped
fresh mint or 2 teaspoons
dried*

1 small garlic clove, minced

*⅛ teaspoon ground cumin, plus
¼ teaspoon for garnish*

¼ teaspoon paprika, for garnish

In a medium bowl, beat the yogurt until it is smooth. Add the cucumber, salt, pepper, mint, garlic, and the ⅛ teaspoon cumin, and stir until well blended. Turn the raita into a serving bowl. Cover with plastic wrap and refrigerate until ready to serve. Just before serving, sprinkle the raita with concentric circles of the cumin and paprika, for garnish. Makes 2½ to 3 cups.

Samosas

Ground Meat or Vegetable Patties

These savory filled pastries are the most popular street snack in India.

Pastry:

3 cups all-purpose flour

1 teaspoon salt

½ cup vegetable oil

½ to ¾ cup cold water

Meat Filling:

2 garlic cloves, halved

1 medium fresh hot green chili, seeded

One 2-inch piece fresh ginger, peeled & coarsely chopped

3 tablespoons vegetable oil

1 teaspoon cumin seeds

1 cup finely chopped onions

2 teaspoons garam masala (p. 93)

1 teaspoon ground turmeric

2 small bay leaves

1 pound ground lamb or beef

1 teaspoon salt

½ cup hot water

Potato Filling:

1 medium fresh hot green chili, seeded

One 2-inch piece fresh ginger, peeled & coarsely chopped

1 tablespoon dried pomegranate seeds (p. 94)

5 tablespoons vegetable oil

½ teaspoon cumin seeds

1 teaspoon coriander seeds, crushed

1 cup finely chopped onions

1½ teaspoons garam masala

1 pound potatoes, peeled, boiled & coarsely chopped

1 cup frozen peas

Vegetable oil for frying

Prepare the Pastry: In a large bowl, combine the flour and salt. Make a well in the center. Pour the oil into the well and rub the mixture between your fingertips until well combined. Add just enough water to make a soft dough. Knead the dough in the bowl 10 minutes, or until smooth and elastic. Shape the dough into a ball, rub lightly with oil, and cover with plastic wrap. Refrigerate 30 minutes.

Prepare the Meat Filling: In a blender, combine the garlic, chili, and ginger, and process to a coarse paste.

In a medium saucepan, heat the oil over high heat until very hot but not smoking. Add the cumin seeds and cook, stirring constantly, 30 seconds, or until the seeds pop and blacken. Reduce the heat to medium and add the onions. Cook, stirring occasionally, 5 minutes, or until lightly browned. Add the chili mixture and cook 1 minute. Stir in the garam masala, turmeric, and bay leaves, and cook 30 seconds. Add the ground meat and salt, and cook, stirring occasionally, 8 minutes. Reduce the heat to medium low, add the water, and simmer, covered, 15 minutes. Uncover and cook 5 minutes, or until all the liquid has evaporated. Discard the bay leaves. Set aside.

Prepare the Potato Filling: In a blender, combine the chili, ginger, and pomegranate seeds, and process to a fine paste.

In a medium saucepan, heat 3 tablespoons of the oil over medium-high heat until very hot but not smoking. Add the cumin and coriander seeds and cook, stirring constantly, 30 seconds, or until the seeds pop and blacken. Add the onions and the remaining oil. Cook, stirring occasionally, 7 minutes, or until the onions are golden brown. Reduce the heat to low, add the chili mixture, and cook, stirring constantly, 4 minutes. Stir in the garam masala, potatoes, and peas, and cook, stirring occasionally, 5 minutes. Set aside.

To make the Samosas: Knead the dough briefly and divide it into 4 portions. Shape each piece into a ball. Work with 1 ball at a time, keeping the remaining dough covered with a clean, damp towel.

Divide 1 ball of dough into 4 pieces. On a lightly floured work surface, roll out each piece into a 6-inch circle. Cut the circle in half. Moisten the edges of one semicircle with cold water and wrap it around your finger to form a cone with a ¼-inch overlapping seam. Press the seam tightly to seal. Loosely fill the cone with 1½ tablespoons of the filling mixture. Pinch the top to seal and crimp the edges with a fork. Set aside on a clean plate. Repeat the process with the remaining dough and filling.

In a deep frying pan, heat 2 inches of oil over medium heat. Using a slotted spoon, place 4 to 5 samosas in the oil and fry 4 to 5 minutes, turning them often, until golden brown. Remove with a slotted spoon and drain on paper towels. Keep warm in a low oven while you fry the remaining samosas. Makes 32.

Pakoras

Vegetable Fritters

Like Samosas (p. 17), Pakoras are a traditional Indian street
food, but nowadays they're normal fare on stylish restaurant menus as well.
These small vegetable fritters made with sweet chick pea flour batter
should be served piping hot. They are wonderful with Pudina Chatni (p. 12).
The filling can vary according to your imagination ~ whole fresh green
chilies, sliced zucchini, fresh fenugreek leaves (p. 93), cauliflower florets, and
sliced bell peppers all are popular alternatives to the vegetables here.

Batter:

*2 cups chick pea flour or gram
flour (p. 93)*

1 cup water

2 garlic cloves, minced

*1 medium fresh hot green chili,
seeded & sliced*

*One 2-inch piece fresh ginger,
peeled & minced*

1 teaspoon salt

1½ teaspoons chili powder

*2 teaspoons garam masala
(p. 93)*

½ teaspoon ground turmeric

*1 tablespoon dried pomegranate
seeds, crushed (p. 94)*

Filling:

*2 cups sliced onions
(¼-inch rings)*

*1 large eggplant, sliced crosswise
into ⅛-inch slices*

*2 cups chopped fresh spinach,
washed & well dried*

*2 cups sliced potatoes
(⅛-inch slices)*

Vegetable oil for deep-frying

Prepare the Batter: Place the flour in a large bowl. Gradually add the water in a thin stream, stirring until smooth. Let stand in a cool place 30 minutes. Stir in the remaining batter ingredients until well combined.

Stir the onions, eggplant, spinach, and pota-

Women carrying ceremonial urns during autumn festival, Jaipur

toes into the batter until well coated.

In a deep skillet, heat the oil to 375°F over medium heat. Add the vegetables in batches and fry turning once, 3 to 4 minutes, or until golden brown and crisp. Drain on paper towels and keep warm in a low oven. Repeat the process with the remaining batter. Makes 30 to 40.

Shami Kebabs

Spicy Lamb Patties

The flavor of roasted split peas lends distinct character to these savory appetizers. Indians have a taste for the earthy crunch of the roasted pea that is much like the Westerners' love for popcorn. They buy handfuls of the snack at outdoor food stalls where the peas are roasted in hot sand over open fire pits, then sifted clean and sold warm. Here the roasted peas are ground into flour, adding subtle richness to this dish. Serve these patties hot as an appetizer or cocktail snack.

½ cup split peas (chana dal)

2 garlic cloves, halved

1 medium fresh hot green chili, seeded

One 2-inch piece fresh ginger, peeled & coarsely chopped

3 tablespoons vegetable oil

1 cup finely chopped onions

2 teaspoons coriander seeds

1 pound lean ground lamb

½ teaspoon salt

1 teaspoon shahi masala (p. 94)

1 teaspoon kalonji (p. 94)

1 teaspoon freshly ground black pepper

¾ cup water

1 large egg, beaten

Flour

Heat a heavy saucepan over medium-low heat. Add the split peas and toast, stirring constantly, 3 to 4 minutes, or until a few peas turn black. Transfer to a plate and allow to cool. In a spice grinder or blender, process the peas until fine. Set aside.

In a blender, combine the garlic, chili, and ginger, and process until fine.

In a large saucepan, heat the oil over medium-high heat. Add the onions and cook, stirring constantly, 6 to 8 minutes, or until lightly browned. Add the garlic mixture and coriander seeds, and cook, stirring constantly, 1 minute. Add the lamb, salt, shahi masala,

kalonji, and pepper, reduce the heat to medium, and cook, stirring constantly, 10 minutes.

Reduce the heat to low, add the water, and cook, covered, 15 minutes. Increase the heat to medium, stir in the ground split peas, and cook, stirring constantly, 2 to 3 minutes, or until all the liquid has evaporated. Allow to cool.

To make the patties, stir the egg into the lamb mixture until well combined. With hands lightly dusted with flour, shape the lamb into 15 to 20 patties about 2 inches in diameter and place on a platter. (If the mixture does not readily form into patties, place in a food processor and process 30 seconds, or until coarsely ground and moist. Cover with plastic wrap and refrigerate 30 minutes before proceeding.)

Preheat the broiler, with the pan 4 inches from the heat source. Broil the patties 5 minutes per side, or until lightly browned. Makes 15 to 20 patties.

Imli Wali Machi

Bluefish Curry with Tamarind

**Tamarind is often used in Indian fish cookery.
Here its sharp flavor offsets the richness of the bluefish.**

*1½ teaspoons tamarind
   concentrate (p. 94)*

¼ cup hot water

1½ cups coarsely chopped onions

2 garlic cloves, halved

*1 medium fresh hot green chili,
   seeded*

*One 2-inch piece fresh ginger,
   peeled & coarsely chopped*

2 tablespoons cold water

¼ cup vegetable oil

1 teaspoon cumin seeds

½ teaspoon chili powder

½ teaspoon ground turmeric

½ teaspoon salt

Pinch of ajowan (p. 92)

*Four 6-ounce bluefish steaks,
   about 2 inches thick*

*3 tablespoons finely chopped
   fresh coriander, for garnish*

In a small bowl, whisk the tamarind and hot water until smooth. Set aside.

In a food processor, combine the onions, garlic, chili, ginger, and cold water, and process to a smooth paste.

In a skillet large enough to hold the fish in a single layer, heat the oil over high heat until very hot but not smoking. Add the cumin seeds and cook, stirring constantly, 30 seconds, or until the seeds pop and blacken. Reduce the heat to low, add the onion mixture, and cook, stirring constantly, 30 seconds. Add the chili powder, turmeric, salt, and ajowan, and cook 1 minute. Add the fish and cook 2 minutes, turning once. Increase the heat to medium and gently stir in the tamarind. Cook, covered, 8 to

10 minutes, or until the fish flakes when tested with a fork and the sauce has thickened. Serve garnished with the fresh coriander. Serves 4.

Kesari Machi

Spicy Baked Fish with Saffron

Almonds and saffron are traditionally associated with Hindu
celebrations of marriages, births, and harvests as well as religious ceremonies.
Here the rich taste of the baked salmon is enhanced by the incomparable
aromatic flavor of saffron, while the almonds add crunchy texture.

Pinch of saffron threads

1 tablespoon hot water

1 tablespoon lemon juice

2 tablespoons slivered blanched
  almonds

1½ tablespoons olive oil

½ teaspoon salt

½ teaspoon freshly ground black
  pepper

1 cup thinly sliced onion rings

One 2-pound salmon, scaled &
  gutted, head & tail left on

2 lemons, quartered, for garnish

In a small bowl, combine the saffron, hot water, and 1½ teaspoons of the lemon juice, and let soak 15 minutes.

Meanwhile, in another small bowl, combine the almonds, 1 tablespoon of the oil, salt, and pepper. In another small bowl, combine the remaining oil and the onions.

Preheat the oven to 400°F. With a sharp knife, score the fish on both sides, making 4 cuts 2 inches long and ¼ inch deep.

Rub the fish inside and out with the saffron and almond mixtures.

Place the fish on an aluminum foil-lined baking sheet. Layer the onion rings on top of the fish. Bake 10 to 15 minutes, or until the fish flakes when tested with a fork. Place on a heated platter and serve immediately, sprinkled with the remaining lemon juice and garnished with lemon wedges. Serves 2.

Nariyal Machi

Fish Steaks in Spicy Coconut Sauce

This recipe is from southern India, where cooking fish
and seafood in coconut sauce is very popular. The blend of mild spices
combines with the coconut to produce a richly delicious, lemon-
yellow sauce that perfectly complements the fish.

2 garlic cloves, halved

1 medium fresh hot green chili,
  seeded

One 2-inch piece fresh ginger,
  peeled & coarsely chopped

4 tablespoons vegetable oil

½ teaspoon cumin seeds

½ teaspoon mustard seeds (p. 94)

1 cup finely chopped onions

1 teaspoon ground coriander

½ teaspoon ground cumin

½ teaspoon ground turmeric

One 13½-ounce can coconut
  milk

½ teaspoon salt

1½ pounds cod, halibut, or
  haddock, cut into four
  1-inch-thick steaks, bone in

2 tablespoons finely chopped
  fresh coriander, for garnish

In a blender, combine the garlic, chili, and ginger, and process until fine. Set aside.

In a skillet large enough to hold the fish in a single layer, heat the oil over high heat until very hot but not smoking. Add the cumin and mustard seeds, and cook stirring constantly, 30 seconds, or until the seeds pop and blacken. Reduce the heat to medium, add the onions, and cook, stirring occasionally, 8 minutes, or until golden.

Reduce the heat to low, stir in the garlic mixture, and cook, stirring constantly, 2 minutes. Add the ground coriander, cumin, and turmeric, and cook, stirring constantly, 1 minute. Stir in the coconut milk and salt. Heat to boiling over high heat, stirring constantly.

Chilies and limes are believed to protect home and property from ill fortune

Add the fish in a single layer and spoon the sauce over. Reduce the heat to low and cook, covered, 4 minutes. Turn the fish carefully and baste with the sauce. Simmer 4 minutes, or until the fish is just tender and flakes when tested with a fork. Serve immediately, garnished with the fresh coriander. Serves 4.

Tomatar Jingha

Spicy Shrimp with Tomatoes

India has over three thousand miles of coastline
and there are numerous regional variations when it comes to cooking
shellfish. This recipe, however, is universally popular, with its light,
aromatic tomato sauce well suited to shrimp.

1 cup chopped onions

4 garlic cloves, halved

*1 medium fresh hot green chili,
    seeded*

2 tablespoons water

4 tablespoons vegetable oil

½ teaspoon chili powder

½ teaspoon ground turmeric

*½ teaspoon garam masala
    (p. 93)*

*1 pound medium shrimp,
    shelled & deveined*

½ teaspoon salt

*4 medium tomatoes,
    peeled & sliced*

1 tablespoon lemon juice

*3 tablespoons finely chopped
    fresh coriander, for garnish*

In a food processor or blender, combine the onion, garlic, chili, and 1 tablespoon of the water, and process until fine.

In a medium saucepan, heat the oil over high heat. Add the onion mixture and cook 8 minutes, or until lightly browned. Reduce the heat to medium, add the chili powder, turmeric, and garam masala, and cook 4 minutes, or until all the liquid has evaporated. Add the shrimp, salt, and the remaining water, and cook, stirring constantly, 3 to 5 minutes, or until the shrimp turn pink. Reduce the heat to low, add the tomatoes, and cook, covered, 8 to 10 minutes, or until the sauce is smooth and thickened. Sprinkle with the lemon juice and serve garnished with the fresh coriander. Serves 4.

Murgh Kari

C h i c k e n   C u r r y

This is the simplest way of cooking chicken in a spicy
sauce and it is prepared all over the subcontinent with slight variations.
In Bengal, for example, tamarind is sometimes added to give extra tanginess,
while in southern India, grated coconut often gives the dish a silken texture.
It is always good served with a fresh salad platter.

4 garlic cloves, halved

2 medium fresh hot green chilies,
    seeded

One 2-inch piece fresh ginger,
    peeled & coarsely chopped

6 to 7 tablespoons water

7 tablespoons vegetable oil

2 cups finely chopped onions

1½ teaspoons ground turmeric

1½ teaspoons ground coriander

1 teaspoon ground cumin

1 teaspoon chili powder

One 3-pound chicken, skin
    removed, cut into 8 pieces

1½ teaspoons salt

4 medium tomatoes, quartered

1 teaspoon garam masala (p. 93)

¼ head lettuce, shredded

1 small cucumber, thinly sliced

2 medium carrots, thinly sliced

2 small onions, thinly sliced in
    rings

2 lemons, cut in wedges

¼ cup finely chopped fresh
    coriander, for garnish

In a blender, combine the garlic, chilies, ginger, and 1 tablespoon water, and process to a fine paste. Set aside.

In a large saucepan, heat the oil over medium-high heat. Add the onions and cook, stirring constantly, 10 minutes, or until a deep golden brown. Add the garlic mixture and cook, stirring constantly, 2 minutes.

Add the turmeric, coriander, cumin, and chili powder, and cook 30 seconds. Add the chicken and salt and turn the chicken to coat well. Cook, stirring constantly, 15 minutes, or until the sauce thickens; add 2 to 3 tablespoons water if necessary to prevent the mixture from sticking to the pan.

Stir in the tomatoes, reduce the heat to medium low, and cook, covered, stirring occasionally, adding 2 to 3 tablespoons water if necessary, about 45 minutes, or until the chicken is just tender. Stir in the garam masala and cook 5 minutes. Arrange the lettuce, cucumber, carrots, onions, and lemons and serve as an accompaniment when chicken is done. Garnish with the coriander. Serves 6.

Murgh Biryani

Chicken Biryani *(picture p. 59)*

Biryani is a favorite at weddings and important banquets and celebrations.

5 large garlic cloves, halved

1 medium fresh hot green chili, seeded

One 2-inch piece fresh ginger, peeled & coarsely chopped

3 tablespoons lemon juice

12 black peppercorns

1 cup plain yogurt

1 teaspoon poppy seeds

1 teaspoon shahi masala (p. 94)

1 teaspoon ground coriander

2 teaspoons ground cumin

½ teaspoon salt

Pinch of ground mace

2 chicken breasts & 2 chicken legs with thighs, skin removed, each cut in 4 pieces

⅓ cup plus 1 tablespoon vegetable oil

12 cloves

4 black cardamom pods, cracked (p. 92)

6 green cardamom pods, cracked

One ½-inch piece cinnamon stick

2 cups finely sliced onion rings

Pinch of saffron threads

3 tablespoons hot milk

2¼ cups basmati rice, rinsed

3 bay leaves

2 tablespoons golden raisins

2 tablespoons sliced almonds, quartered lengthwise, for garnish

2 hard-boiled eggs, quartered lengthwise & halved crosswise, for garnish

In a food processor or blender, combine the garlic, chili, ginger, lemon juice, and peppercorns, and process to a coarse paste. Transfer to a large bowl and add the yogurt, poppy seeds, shahi masala, coriander, cumin, salt, and mace. Stir until well combined.

With a fork, prick the chicken pieces. Add to the yogurt marinade and toss until well coated. Cover with plastic wrap and let stand 2 hours.

In a large saucepan, heat ⅓ cup oil over high heat until very hot but not smoking. Add the cloves, cardamom pods, and cinnamon, and cook, stirring constantly, 30 seconds. Reduce the heat to medium, add 1½ cups of the onions, and cook, stirring frequently, 8 minutes, or until the onions are lightly browned. Add the chicken and marinade and heat to boiling over high heat. Reduce the heat to low and cook, covered, 15 minutes.

Meanwhile, preheat the oven to 300°F.

Heat a small skillet over medium-high heat. Add the saffron and toast, stirring constantly, 15 seconds. In a small bowl, crumble the saffron into the milk. Let stand 15 minutes. In a large saucepan, cook the rice in boiling water 2 minutes. Drain thoroughly in a fine sieve.

In a Dutch oven, combine the rice, chicken, and bay leaves. Drizzle the saffron milk over the mixture and toss with a fork. Cover with aluminum foil and a tight-fitting lid and bake 30 minutes, or until the rice is tender.

Meanwhile, in a medium skillet, heat the 1 tablespoon oil over medium heat. Add the remaining onion and cook 10 minutes, or until browned; transfer to a plate. Add the raisins and almonds to the pan, and cook 3 to 4 minutes, or until the nuts are lightly golden.

Spoon the biryani onto a heated serving platter. Top with the onions, raisins, and nuts. Garnish with the eggs. Serves 6 to 8.

Masala Murgha

Spicy Whole Baked Chicken

This simple roast chicken ~ flavorful but not too fiery ~ is a lovely light supper or lunch dish. Serve with Mattar Chaval (p. 79) and Kheere ka Raita (p. 16).

3 large garlic cloves, halved

1 medium fresh hot green chili, seeded

One 2-inch piece fresh ginger, peeled & coarsely chopped

¼ cup fresh coriander leaves

2 tablespoons lemon juice

1 teaspoon ground turmeric

1 teaspoon ground cumin

1½ teaspoons sweet paprika or 1 teaspoon red food coloring

½ teaspoon salt

2 tablespoons vegetable oil

One 3- to 3½-pound chicken, skin removed

1 tablespoon unsalted butter, softened

For Garnish:

6 sprigs fresh coriander

2 lemons, sliced

2 large tomatoes, cut in wedges

½ cucumber, thinly sliced

1 small onion, thinly sliced

In a blender, combine the garlic, chili, ginger, coriander, and lemon juice, and process to a fine paste. Transfer to small bowl and add the turmeric, cumin, paprika, salt, and oil. Stir to make a coarse paste.

Using a sharp knife, score the chicken in several places and place in a shallow baking dish. Rub the spice paste over the chicken, spreading it into the crevices, until the bird is evenly covered; rub some of the paste inside the cavity. Cover the chicken with plastic wrap and refrigerate at least 3 hours, or overnight.

Preheat the oven to 400°F. Place the

chicken on a rack in a roasting pan. Dot the surface with the butter. Bake, basting with the pan juices several times, 1½ hours, or until the juices run clear when the chicken is pierced with a fork.

Transfer the chicken to a serving platter and garnish with the coriander sprigs, lemons, tomatoes, cucumber, and onion. Serves 4.

Tandoori Murgha

Tandoori-Style Chicken

Named for the blazing-hot tandoor (clay) oven in which the dish is
traditionally baked ~ in only 5 minutes ~ this spicy chicken is just as delicious
grilled or broiled. The red coloring symbolizes good luck and fortune.

Marinade:

1 teaspoon ground coriander

1 teaspoon ground cumin

1 teaspoon ground turmeric

½ teaspoon asafetida (p. 92)

2 teaspoons chili powder

1 tablespoon shahi masala
 (p. 94)

½ teaspoon red food coloring
 powder (optional)

1 teaspoon salt

6 tablespoons plain yogurt

4 chicken breasts, skin removed

1 tablespoon unsalted butter,
 softened

For Garnish:

2 medium tomatoes, sliced

2 lemons, quartered

¾ cup thinly sliced onion rings

In a small bowl, combine all the marinade ingredients. With a sharp knife, score the chicken breasts in several places and place them in a shallow baking dish. Pour the marinade over the chicken and rub it into each piece. Cover with plastic wrap and let stand 2 hours, turning the chicken every 30 minutes, or refrigerate overnight.

Preheat a barbecue or broiler to high heat. Grill or broil the chicken, basting often with the marinade, 20 minutes on each side, or until well browned. To serve, spread the butter over the chicken, and garnish with the tomatoes, lemons, and onion. Serves 4.

Tandoori Murgha, Mattar Chaval, page 79,
Kheere ka Raita, page 16 & Bhindi Bhaji, page 57

Murgh Dhansak

Chicken with Vegetables and Lentils

A Parsee delicacy, this main course enjoys the same status in that
Indian community as does a Sunday roast in the West. Fresh fenugreek is the
secret ingredient, adding a pungent aroma and slightly bitter taste.

8 garlic cloves, halved

8 medium fresh hot green chilies,
seeded

One 2-inch piece fresh ginger,
peeled & coarsely chopped

1½ teaspoons cumin seeds

1½ teaspoons coriander seeds

One 3-inch cinnamon stick

10 black peppercorns

10 cloves

2 tablespoons red lentils (masoor
dal), rinsed & picked over

2 tablespoons mung beans (mung
dal), rinsed & picked over

2 tablespoons pigeon peas (toovar
dal), rinsed & picked over

One 3-pound chicken, skin
removed, cut into 8 pieces

½ pound butternut squash,
peeled & cut into 1-inch
pieces

1½ cups coarsely chopped
eggplant

½ cup coarsely chopped carrot

1 cup finely chopped fresh fenugreek (p. 93) or spinach leaves

2 cups water

½ cup vegetable oil

2 cups sliced onions

2 cups roughly chopped peeled
tomatoes

3 tablespoons finely chopped
fresh coriander

1 tablespoon jaggery (p. 93) or
light brown sugar

½ teaspoon salt

In a food processor or blender, combine the garlic, chilies, ginger, cumin and coriander seeds,
cinnamon, peppercorns, and cloves, and process to a coarse paste. Set aside.

In a large saucepan, combine the lentils, mung beans, pigeon peas, chicken, squash, eggplant, carrot, fenugreek, and water. Heat to boiling, reduce the heat to medium low, and cook, covered, 30 minutes, or until all the beans are tender.

Meanwhile, in a medium saucepan, heat the oil over high heat. Add the onions and cook, stirring constantly, 10 minutes, or until golden brown. Reduce the heat to medium, add the garlic mixture, and cook 1 minute. Stir in the tomatoes, fresh coriander, jaggery, and salt. Cook, stirring constantly, 2 minutes. Remove from the heat.

Using a slotted spoon, transfer the chicken to a plate. In a food processor, working in batches if necessary, process the cooking liquid and vegetables to a rough purée. Add the purée to the onion mixture, and heat to boiling over medium heat. Add the chicken pieces, reduce the heat, and simmer 5 to 10 minutes, or until the chicken is warmed through. Serves 6 to 8.

Murgh Makhan

Silken Chicken

The Mughals, who ruled India for almost three hundred years, loved eating and entertaining, and rich, creamy dishes such as this formed an essential part of their lavish lifestyle. Serve this very special dish as part of a large meal.

4 garlic cloves, halved

1 medium fresh hot green chili, seeded

One 2-inch piece fresh ginger, peeled & coarsely chopped

2 cups finely chopped onions

8 cardamom pods, cracked (p. 92)

9 cloves

8 tablespoons (1 stick) unsalted butter

1 tablespoon vegetable oil

One 3-pound chicken, skin removed, cut into 10 pieces

2 teaspoons cumin seeds

1 teaspoon chili powder

One 1½-inch piece cinnamon stick

One 16-ounce can whole tomatoes, chopped, with juice

½ teaspoon salt

¼ cup finely chopped fresh coriander, for garnish

In a food processor, combine the garlic, chili, and ginger, and process 15 seconds. Add the onions and process 15 seconds. Add the cardamom pods and cloves, and process 15 seconds. Set aside.

In a large saucepan, heat 3 tablespoons of the butter and the oil over high heat until foamy. When the foam has almost subsided, reduce the heat to medium, add half the chicken, and cook, turning often, 10 minutes, or until lightly browned on all sides. Transfer the chicken to a plate. Add 3 tablespoons more butter to the pan and repeat the process with the remaining chicken.

Add the remaining butter and the garlic mixture to the pan, and cook, stirring constantly, 8 minutes, or until the liquid has evaporated. Add the cumin seeds, chili powder, and cinnamon stick, and cook, stirring constantly, 2 minutes. Add the tomatoes and salt, and cook, stirring frequently, 10 minutes. Add the chicken and its juices, reduce the heat to low, and cook, covered, 30 minutes, or until the chicken is tender and the sauce has thickened. Garnish with the fresh coriander. Serves 6.

Sag Gosht

Lamb with Spinach

Spinach and lamb make good companions ~ the juices of the meat and the earthy flavor of the vegetable produce a well-balanced dish. This rendition is especially popular in Nepal and Sri Lanka.

¼ cup plus 1 tablespoon vegetable oil

2 pounds boneless lean lamb (leg or shoulder), cut into 1-inch pieces

1 teaspoon fenugreek seeds (p. 93)

½ teaspoon cumin seeds

1 teaspoon black mustard seeds (p. 94)

One 3-inch cinnamon stick

6 cardamom pods (p. 92)

2 cups coarsely chopped onions

6 garlic cloves, halved

1 large fresh hot green chili, seeded

One 2-inch piece fresh ginger, peeled & coarsely chopped

2 teaspoons ground turmeric

1 teaspoon ground cumin

1 teaspoon chili powder

1 teaspoon ground coriander

2 bay leaves

2 tablespoons water

1½ pounds frozen spinach

1 teaspoon salt

¼ cup finely chopped fresh coriander, for garnish

In a large saucepan, heat 2 tablespoons of the oil over high heat. Add half the lamb and cook, turning often, 6 minutes, or until lightly browned on all sides. Transfer the lamb to a plate. Add 1 tablespoon oil to the pan and repeat the process with the remaining lamb.

Add 2 tablespoons oil to the pan and heat until very hot but not smoking. Add the fenugreek, cumin and mustard seeds, cinnamon, and cardamom, and cook, stirring

Sag Gosht & Sabji ka Chaval, page 81

constantly, 1 minute, or until the seeds pop and blacken. Reduce the heat to medium, add the onions, and cook, stirring occasionally, 5 minutes, or until the onions are soft.

Meanwhile, in a blender, combine the garlic, chili, and ginger, and process until fine.

Add the garlic mixture, turmeric, ground cumin, chili powder, ground coriander, and bay leaves to the onions, and cook, stirring constantly, 1 minute. Add the water, spinach, and salt, and cook, covered, stirring often, 15 minutes, or until the spinach is tender. Reduce the heat to low and cook, covered, stirring occasionally, 1½ hours, or until the lamb is tender. Serve garnished with the fresh coriander. Serves 6 to 8.

Seekh Kebab

Spiced Grilled Ground Beef or Lamb

These kebabs taste best hot off the grill. Serve them as
cocktail snacks or, with salad, as a light starter. The ground meat can be mixed
with the spices a day ahead of time and refrigerated overnight to marinate.
Allow to come to room temperature before grilling.

2 garlic cloves, halved

1 medium fresh hot green chili,
   seeded

One 1-inch piece fresh ginger,
   peeled & coarsely chopped

1 pound ground beef or lamb

½ teaspoon salt

1 teaspoon tandoori masala
   (p. 94)

½ teaspoon ground turmeric

½ teaspoon chili powder

1 teaspoon cornstarch

1 large egg yolk

1 tablespoon vegetable oil

For Garnish:

2 lemons or limes, quartered

¾ cup thinly sliced onion rings

2 tomatoes, quartered

In a blender, combine the garlic, chili, and ginger, and process until fine. Transfer to a large bowl and add the meat, salt, tandoori masala, turmeric, chili powder, and cornstarch, and toss to combine. Stir in the egg yolk and oil until well combined. Cover and let stand 2 hours, or refrigerate overnight.

Preheat a barbecue grill to medium heat.

Working with wet hands, shape the meat mixture into 8 equal balls and roll each between your fingers into 6-inch long sausages. Thread the meat onto 4 metal skewers.

Grill the kebabs 7 to 8 minutes per side, or until lightly browned. Transfer to a heated serving platter and garnish with the lemons, onion, and tomatoes. Serves 4.

Keema Mattar

Spicy Ground Beef with Peas

This is a very easy and economical side dish. It is versatile
as well ~ you can vary the spices according to taste and adjust the heat by
adding more or less fresh chili. An additional tablespoon of lemon or
lime juice can be substituted for the dried mango powder.

3 garlic cloves, halved

*1 large fresh hot green chili,
seeded*

*One 2-inch piece fresh ginger,
peeled*

5 tablespoons vegetable oil

1 teaspoon cumin seeds

*1 teaspoon black mustard seeds
(p. 94)*

1½ cups coarsely chopped onions

2 bay leaves

One 3-inch cinnamon stick

1 teaspoon ground turmeric

1 teaspoon chili powder

1 teaspoon ground cumin

1 teaspoon ground coriander

1 pound ground beef

1 cup water

*2 medium tomatoes, coarsely
chopped*

1 teaspoon salt

1 cup fresh or thawed frozen peas

1 teaspoon garam masala (p. 93)

1 tablespoon lemon juice

*Pinch of dried mango powder
(p. 94)*

*2 tablespoons finely chopped
fresh coriander, for garnish*

In a blender, combine the garlic, chili, and ginger, and process until fine. Set aside.

In a medium saucepan, heat the oil over high heat until very hot but not smoking. Add the cumin and mustard seeds, and cook, stirring, 30 seconds, or until the seeds pop. Reduce the heat to medium, add the onions, and cook, stirring occasionally, 10 minutes,

Keema Mattar, Chapatis, page 82, Masoor Dal, page 76,
Kachoomber, page 15, Kheere ka Raita, page 16 & Sada Chaval, page 78

or until golden. Stir in the garlic mixture and cook 1 minute. Add the bay leaves, cinnamon, turmeric, chili powder, ground cumin, ground coriander, and beef, and cook, stirring occasionally, 10 minutes. Add the water, tomatoes, and salt, and cook 5 minutes. Reduce the heat to low, add the peas, and cook, stirring occasionally, 10 to 15 minutes, or until the peas are tender. Stir in the garam masala, lemon juice, and mango powder. Serve garnished with the fresh coriander. Serves 4.

Shahi Korma

Braised Lamb in Yogurt Sauce

**Versions of this lightly spiced, aromatic dish
are popular throughout India. It can also be made with beef.**

6 garlic cloves, halved

1 medium fresh hot green chili,
　seeded

One 2-inch piece fresh ginger,
　peeled & coarsely chopped

1 tablespoon plus 1 cup water

2 cups coarsely chopped onions

½ cup vegetable oil

6 cloves

6 green cardamom pods, cracked
　(p. 92)

10 black peppercorns

One 3-inch cinnamon stick

2 pounds boneless lean lamb
　(leg or shoulder), cut into
　2-inch pieces

2 teaspoons ground coriander

1 teaspoon chili powder

½ teaspoon shahi masala (p. 94)

1 teaspoon salt

1 bay leaf

1 cup plain yogurt

In a blender, combine the garlic, chili, and ginger, and process 30 seconds, or until fine. Add the 1 tablespoon water and the onions, and process to a smooth paste. Set aside.

In a large saucepan, heat the oil over high heat until very hot but not smoking. Add the cloves, cardamom, peppercorns, and cinnamon, and cook, stirring constantly, 30 seconds. Reduce the heat to medium, add the lamb, and cook, stirring often, 8 to 10 minutes, or until the lamb is well browned on all sides. Stir in the onion mixture, ground coriander, chili powder, shahi masala, salt, and bay leaf, and cook, stirring frequently, 8 to 10 minutes, adding a tablespoon or so of water if necessary to prevent

The Water Palace of Jal Mahal near the ancient capital of Amber

the mixture from sticking to the pan.

Increase the heat to high and add the yogurt a tablespoon at a time, stirring well after each addition. Cook, stirring occasionally, 8 to 10 minutes, or until the liquid has evaporated. Add ½ cup water and stir until well blended. Add the remaining water and heat to boiling, stirring constantly. Reduce the heat to low and cook, covered, 1½ hours, or until the lamb is tender. Serves 4 to 6.

Rogon Josh

Lamb Lahore

This is the most popular northern Indian meat dish.
The recipe calls for lamb on the bone because it adds flavor and keeps
the meat succulent during cooking; ask your butcher to cut the lamb into
1-inch slices. You can, of course, use boneless meat.

4 garlic cloves, halved

2 medium fresh hot green chilies,
seeded

One 2-inch piece fresh ginger,
peeled & coarsely chopped

5 tablespoons vegetable oil

2½ cups finely chopped onions

1 teaspoon ground turmeric

1 teaspoon chili powder

1 teaspoon ground cumin

1 teaspoon ground coriander

2 pounds leg of lamb, bone in,
sliced, or 1 pound boneless
lamb, cut into 1-inch cubes

One 3-inch cinnamon stick

2 bay leaves

½ teaspoon salt

4 tomatoes, peeled & quartered

1 teaspoon garam masala (p. 93)

1 tablespoon lime juice

¼ cup fresh coriander leaves,
for garnish

In a blender, combine the garlic, chilies, and ginger, and process until fine. Set aside.

In a large saucepan, heat the oil over medium-high heat. Add the onions and cook, stirring frequently, 15 minutes, or until dark golden brown. Stir in the turmeric, chili powder, cumin, and ground coriander, and cook, stirring constantly, 30 seconds. Reduce the heat to medium, add the garlic mixture, and cook, stirring constantly, 30 seconds. Add the lamb, cinnamon, bay leaves, and salt, and cook, stirring occasionally, 15 minutes, or until the lamb is well browned; add 1 to 3 table-

Rogon Josh & Kesari Chaval, page 80

spoons water if necessary to prevent the mixture from sticking to the pan.

Reduce the heat to low, add the tomatoes, and cook, covered, stirring occasionally, 1¼ to 1½ hours, or until the lamb is tender; add

water if necessary to prevent the mixture from sticking to the pan.

Stir in the garam masala and cook 5 minutes. Just before serving, stir in the lime juice. Garnish with the fresh coriander. Serves 4.

Vindaloo

Goan-Style Pork

This powerfully flavored dish from the Christian community of Goa in western India is traditionally made with pork, though lamb or beef can be substituted. For the most flavorful results, marinate the meat overnight.

1½ teaspoons tamarind concentrate (p. 94)

¼ cup hot water

½ teaspoon cumin seeds

½ teaspoon black mustard seeds (p. 94)

½ teaspoon coriander seeds

2 bay leaves

One 3-inch cinnamon stick

½ teaspoon black peppercorns

6 garlic cloves, halved

2 medium fresh hot green chilies, seeded

One 2-inch piece fresh ginger, peeled & coarsely chopped

2 tablespoons plus ½ cup olive oil

2 pounds boneless lean pork (leg or shoulder), cut in 1-inch cubes

½ cup thinly sliced onions plus 1 cup finely chopped onions for garnish

1½ teaspoons ground turmeric

½ teaspoon cracked fenugreek seeds (p. 93)

2 teaspoons chili powder

1½ teaspoons ground coriander

½ teaspoon salt

½ cup apple cider vinegar or distilled white vinegar

¼ cup water

2 tablespoons vegetable oil

¼ cup finely chopped fresh coriander, for garnish

In a small bowl, whisk the tamarind and hot water until smooth. Set aside.

Heat a heavy skillet over medium heat. Add the cumin, mustard, and coriander seeds, and

toast, stirring constantly, 4 minutes, or until they begin to pop. In a spice grinder or a mortar with pestle, grind the seeds, bay leaves, cinnamon, and peppercorns until fine. Transfer to a small bowl.

In a blender, combine the garlic, chilies, and ginger, and process until fine. Stir the garlic mixture, and the 2 tablespoons olive oil, into the ground spices. Place the pork in a large bowl, add the garlic-spice mixture and the tamarind, and toss until well coated. Cover with plastic wrap and let stand 2 hours, or refrigerate overnight.

In a large skillet, heat the ½ cup olive oil over medium-high heat. Add the sliced onion and cook, stirring frequently, 10 minutes, or until lightly browned. Add the turmeric, fenugreek, chili powder, ground coriander, and salt, and cook, stirring constantly, 30 seconds. Reduce the heat to medium, add the pork and its marinade, and cook, turning the pork often, 5 minutes. Reduce the heat to low and cook, stirring occasionally, 10 minutes. Stir in the cider vinegar and cook, covered, stirring occasionally, 30 minutes. Stir in the water and cook, covered, 1¼ to 1½ hours, or until the pork is tender.

Meanwhile, in a small skillet, heat the vegetable oil over high heat. Add the remaining chopped onions and cook, stirring constantly, 12 minutes, or until brown and crispy.

Serve the Vindaloo garnished with the onions and fresh coriander. Serves 6 to 8.

Bhindi Bhaji

F r i e d   S t u f f e d   O k r a   *(picture p. 39)*

This slim and elegant-looking vegetable grows all over India,
from the foothills of the Himalayas in the North to Madura in the South.
It has a subtle flavor enhanced by the spices here. Serve as part of a
vegetarian meal with dal, rice, bread, raita, and chutney.

*1 tablespoon plus 1 teaspoon
   chili powder*

2 teaspoons ground turmeric

2 teaspoons ground coriander

½ teaspoon salt

1 pound okra, trimmed

6 tablespoons vegetable oil

1½ cups roughly chopped onions

1 tablespoon water (optional)

*¼ cup finely chopped fresh
   coriander, for garnish*

2 lemons, quartered, for garnish

In a small bowl, combine the chili powder, turmeric, coriander, and salt. With a small sharp knife, cut a lengthwise slit in each okra pod, taking care not to cut completely through. Stuff each pod with a little of the spice mixture.

In a medium saucepan, heat the oil over high heat. Add the onions and cook, stirring constantly, 12 minutes, or until browned. Reduce the heat to low and add the okra. Add the water if the mixture seems too dry. Cook, covered, 10 minutes, or until the okra is tender but still retains its color. Serve garnished with the fresh coriander and lemons. Serves 4.

Barbatti Nariyal Sabji

Green Beans with Fresh Coconut

This light vegetable dish is typical of the cooking of
southern India, where coconuts grow abundantly. If you can't find
fresh coconut, the dried unsweetened coconut available at
health food stores is a good substitute.

⅓ cup grated fresh coconut or
 dried unsweetened coconut

2 tablespoons finely chopped
 fresh coriander

1 medium fresh hot green chili,
 seeded & finely chopped

½ teaspoon salt

¼ cup vegetable oil

1 tablespoon sesame seeds

1 teaspoon black mustard seeds
 (p. 94)

Pinch of ground coriander

Pinch of chili powder

Pinch of ground turmeric

1 pound haricots verts or thin
 young green beans, trimmed,
 cut in 2-inch pieces &
 steamed until just
 crisp-tender

In a medium bowl, combine the coconut, fresh coriander, chili, and salt. Set aside.

In a large saucepan, heat the oil over high heat until very hot but not smoking. Add the sesame and mustard seeds, and cook, stirring constantly, 1 minute, or until they begin to pop. Stir in the ground coriander, chili powder, and turmeric, and cook 15 seconds. Reduce the heat to medium, add the beans and the coconut mixture, and cook, stirring constantly, 6 minutes, or until the beans are tender. Serve immediately. Serves 4.

Barbatti Nariyal Sabji & Murgh Biryani, page 34

Baingan Bharta

Roasted Eggplant

This is a particularly popular dish in northern
and central India, where usually the eggplants are charbroiled
over a wood fire or in the tandoor before being mashed and mixed
with flavorings. This method produces a strong smoky flavor,
and the chili and spices add a piquant bite.

2 large eggplants

2 garlic cloves, halved

1 large fresh hot green chili,
    seeded

One 2-inch piece fresh ginger,
    peeled & coarsely chopped

4 tablespoons vegetable oil

4 cardamom pods (p. 92)

2 cloves

1 cup finely chopped onions

½ teaspoon ground turmeric

½ teaspoon ground coriander

½ teaspoon chili powder

1 tablespoon finely chopped fresh
    coriander, plus 1 tablespoon
    for garnish

1 tablespoon lime juice, optional

1 teaspoon garam masala
    (p. 93)

2 medium tomatoes, roughly
    sliced, plus 1 tomato sliced,
    for garnish

Preheat the broiler, with the pan 6 inches from the heat source. Broil the eggplants, turning often, 25 minutes, or until tender and the skin is well charred. Transfer to a paper bag and let stand 10 minutes; peel and discard skin. In a large bowl, mash the eggplant to a coarse pulp. Set aside.

In a blender, combine the garlic, chili, and ginger, and process until fine. Set aside.

In a medium saucepan, heat the oil over high heat until very hot but not smoking. Add the cardamom and cloves, and cook, stirring con-

stantly, 1 minute. Reduce the heat to medium low, add the onions, and cook, stirring occasionally, 10 minutes, or until golden brown. Stir in the garlic mixture, turmeric, ground coriander, and chili powder until well combined. Cook, stirring occasionally, 2 minutes.

Reduce the heat to low, add the eggplant and fresh coriander, and cook 10 minutes. Add the 2 tomatoes and cook 5 minutes longer. Stir in the lime juice if desired and sprinkle with the garam masala. Serve garnished with the fresh coriander and sliced tomato. Serves 4.

Aloo Mattar Gajar

Spicy Carrots, Peas, and Potatoes

A simple recipe using ingredients found in most kitchens, this dish
is prepared throughout India. Serve with Sag Gosht (p. 44), Kheere ka Raita (p. 16),
and a salad platter of lettuce, tomatoes, cucumber, carrots, and onion.

5 tablespoons vegetable oil

1 teaspoon cumin seeds

1 cup thinly sliced onions

½ teaspoon ground turmeric

½ teaspoon chili powder

½ teaspoon ground coriander

½ teaspoon salt

*1 pound new potatoes, peeled &
cut in ¼-inch slices*

*½ pound carrots, cut in ¼-inch
slices*

2 to 3 tablespoons water

1 cup frozen peas, thawed

*¼ cup finely chopped fresh
coriander, for garnish*

In a large skillet, heat 1 tablespoon of the oil over high heat until very hot but not smoking. Add the cumin seeds and cook, stirring constantly, 30 seconds, or until they pop and blacken. Reduce the heat to medium, add the remaining oil and the onions, and cook 10 minutes, or until the onions are lightly browned.

Stir in the turmeric, chili, coriander, and salt. Reduce the heat to low, add the potatoes and carrots, and toss until the vegetables are coated with the spices. Cook, covered, 15 minutes. Stir in 2 tablespoons water and cook 5 minutes longer, adding 1 more tablespoon water if the mixture sticks to the pan. Stir in the peas and cook, covered, 5 minutes, or until tender. Serve garnished with the fresh coriander. Serves 4.

Aloo Ghobi

Braised Spicy Cauliflower with Potatoes

**Potatoes and cauliflower make an ideal partnership,
their flavors complementing each other perfectly; here they are spiked
with cumin seeds and nutty brown onions.**

5 tablespoons vegetable oil

1 tablespoon cumin seeds

3 garlic cloves, minced

*1 fresh hot green chili, seeded &
thinly sliced*

*One 2-inch piece fresh ginger,
peeled & cut into very thin
slivers*

½ teaspoon chili powder

½ teaspoon ground coriander

½ teaspoon ground turmeric

*1 medium cauliflower, trimmed
& cut into florets*

1 teaspoon salt

*1 large potato, peeled & cut into
1-inch cubes*

*1 teaspoon garam masala
(p. 93)*

*¼ cup finely chopped fresh
coriander, for garnish*

*2 tomatoes, thinly sliced, for
garnish*

In a large saucepan, heat the oil over high heat until very hot but not smoking. Add the cumin seeds and cook, stirring constantly, 30 seconds, or until they pop and blacken. Reduce the heat to low, add the garlic, chili, and ginger, and cook, stirring constantly, 5 minutes, or until fragrant. Stir in the chili powder, ground coriander, turmeric, cauliflower, and salt, and cook, covered, 10 minutes. Gently stir in the potatoes and 1 to 2 tablespoons water to prevent the mixture from sticking. Cook, covered, 20 minutes.

To serve, sprinkle with the garam masala and garnish with the coriander and tomatoes. Serves 4.

Aloo Bhaji

Braised Potatoes with Tomatoes

The tomatoes add color to this quick and easy dish
as well as a sharpness that balances the potatoes and spices.

3 garlic cloves, halved

One 1-inch piece fresh ginger,
    peeled & coarsely chopped

6 tablespoons vegetable oil

1½ cups minced onions

1 medium fresh hot green chili,
    seeded & sliced

1 pound potatoes, peeled & cut
    into 2-inch pieces

4 medium tomatoes, cut into
    quarters

1 teaspoon cumin seeds

1 teaspoon ground turmeric

1 teaspoon ground coriander

1 teaspoon ground cumin

1 teaspoon chili powder

1 teaspoon salt

Pinch of ajowan seeds (p. 92)

1 teaspoon garam masala (p. 93)

¼ cup finely chopped fresh
    coriander, for garnish

In a blender, combine the garlic and ginger, and process until fine. Set aside.

In a large saucepan, heat the oil over medium-high heat. Add the onions and cook, stirring occasionally, 10 minutes, or until browned. Reduce the heat to medium, add the garlic mixture and the chili, and cook, stirring constantly, 1 minute. Add the potatoes and cook 5 minutes. Reduce the heat to medium low and add the tomatoes, cumin seeds, turmeric, ground coriander, ground cumin, chili powder, salt, and ajowan. Cook, covered, 20 minutes, or until the potatoes are tender. To serve, sprinkle with the garam masala and garnish with fresh coriander. Serves 4.

Malai Baingan

Spiced Baby Eggplant with Cream

This is a deliciously creamy and delicately spiced dish, perfect on special occasions as part of a light lunch or a celebratory dinner. Serve with Tandoori Murgha (p. 38), Hare Dhaniya ki Chatni (p. 13), and Chapatis (p. 82).

6 tablespoons vegetable oil

1 teaspoon cumin seeds

Pinch of coriander seeds

1 cup thinly sliced onions

½ teaspoon ground turmeric

½ teaspoon chili powder

½ teaspoon ground coriander

1 pound baby eggplant, trimmed & cut lengthwise in ½-inch-thick slices

½ red bell pepper, sliced in strips

½ teaspoon salt

⅓ cup heavy cream

2 tablespoons finely chopped fresh coriander, for garnish

In a medium saucepan, heat 2 tablespoons of the oil over high heat until very hot but not smoking. Add the cumin and coriander seeds, and cook 30 seconds, or until they pop and blacken. Reduce the heat to medium, add the onions, and cook, stirring frequently, 10 minutes, or until lightly browned. Stir in the turmeric, chili powder, and ground coriander, and cook 1 minute longer.

Add the remaining oil, the eggplant, bell pepper, and salt. Cook, stirring occasionally, 6 minutes, or until the vegetables are tender. Remove from the heat and gently stir in the cream. Serve immediately, garnished with the fresh coriander. Serves 4.

Panir

This slightly crumbly fresh cheese is used in many sweet
dishes and desserts and in savory dishes such as Mattar Panir (p. 70).
It keeps in the refrigerator for up to 2 days.

2 quarts milk

4 tablespoons lemon juice

In a large heavy saucepan, heat the milk to boiling over high heat, stirring constantly to prevent scorching. Reduce the heat to low, add the lemon juice, and stir very gently 15 to 20 seconds. Remove the pan from the heat and continue stirring 1 minute, or until soft curds form. If curds are slow to form, return the pan to low heat for a few seconds. Set aside for 15 minutes.

Line a colander with cheesecloth or a large white linen handkerchief and place it in the sink or over a bowl. Pour the curdled milk mixture into the colander. Gently rinse under cold water for 10 seconds to remove the acidic flavor of the lemon juice.

Pull up the corners of the cheesecloth, twist them together, and tie the ends to make a bag. Hang the curd over a bowl to drain 4 hours at room temperature, or overnight in the refrigerator.

Loosen the ends of the cloth and place the loosely wrapped "sack" of cheese on a large plate. Weight down the cheese with a heavy bowl or plate, pressing it to about ¾-inch thick. Refrigerate at least 4 hours before using. Makes about 1½ cups.

Mattar Panir

Homemade Cottage Cheese with Peas and Tomatoes

This northern Indian dish features freshly made
panir although ready-made panir, available from some Indian stores,
is an acceptable substitute. Serve as part of a vegetarian meal with
another vegetable dish, dal, rice, and Indian bread.

7 tablespoons vegetable oil

1 teaspoon cumin seeds

¾ cup finely chopped onion

1 teaspoon ground coriander

½ teaspoon ground turmeric

½ teaspoon chili powder

½ teaspoon ground cumin

½ teaspoon salt

1 large tomato, peeled & thinly
sliced

12 ounces Panir (p. 69), cut into
½-inch cubes

2½ cups frozen peas, thawed

1 cup water

1 teaspoon garam masala (p. 93)

¼ cup finely chopped fresh
coriander, for garnish

In a large skillet, heat 3 tablespoons of the oil over high heat until very hot but not smoking. Add the cumin seeds and cook, stirring constantly, 30 seconds, or until the seeds pop and blacken. Reduce the heat to medium, add the onion, and cook, stirring occasionally, 10 minutes, or until well browned. Add the ground coriander, turmeric, chili powder, ground cumin, and salt, and cook,

stirring constantly, 45 seconds. Reduce the heat to low, add the tomato, and cook, covered, stirring occasionally, 15 minutes, or until the sauce thickens.

Meanwhile, in a medium nonstick skillet, heat the remaining oil over medium heat. Add the panir and cook, stirring often, until lightly browned. Transfer to paper towels to drain.

Stir the peas, panir, and water into the onion mixture and cook 5 minutes. To serve, stir in the garam masala and garnish with the coriander. Serves 4 to 6.

Rajma

Royal Beans

Called "royal beans" because of their rich flavor, this nutritious
everyday recipe is a great favorite with Punjabis and other peoples of northern India.

*2 cups dried red kidney beans,
  rinsed & picked over*

1 cup chopped onions

4 garlic cloves, finely chopped

*One 2-inch piece fresh ginger,
  peeled & coarsely chopped*

1 teaspoon ground turmeric

1 teaspoon ground coriander

1 teaspoon chili powder

1 teaspoon ground cumin

1 teaspoon cumin seeds

1 teaspoon mustard seeds (p. 94)

1 teaspoon asafetida (p. 92)

⅓ cup oil

*One 16-ounce can whole
  tomatoes, chopped, with juice*

1 teaspoon salt

*¼ cup finely chopped fresh
  coriander, for garnish*

In a medium bowl, soak the beans in 4 cups water at least 8 hours or overnight. Drain; reserve the soaking water and add enough fresh water to make a total of 6 cups.

In a 4-quart pressure cooker, combine the beans, the 6 cups water, the onions, garlic, ginger, the spices, and oil. Heat to boiling, cover, and cook 15 minutes at 15 pounds pressure, according to manufac-turer's instructions. Remove from the heat and reduce pressure quickly, according to manufacturer's instructions.

Remove the lid and stir in the tomatoes and salt. Heat to boiling, cover, and cook 20 minutes at 15 pounds pressure, or until the beans are soft. Serve garnished with the fresh coriander. Serves 8.

Kali Dal

Spicy Black Lentils or Urad

This dish is made with whole black urad dal, also known as
black gram. This type of dal is also available split, which cooks
in less time, but using the whole bean results in a richer, smoother texture.
Dal takes a long time to cook, but a pressure cooker speeds up the process.
Serve as part of a vegetarian meal with rice and bread.

*2 cups black lentils (urad dal),
rinsed & picked over*

4 garlic cloves, halved

*3 medium fresh hot green chilies,
seeded*

*One 2-inch piece fresh ginger,
peeled & roughly chopped*

6 to 8 cups water

1½ cups roughly chopped onions

1½ teaspoons ground turmeric

1½ teaspoons ground coriander

1 teaspoon ground cumin

1 teaspoon chili powder

2 bay leaves

1½ teaspoons cumin seeds

2 pinches of asafetida (p. 92)

1 teaspoon salt

¼ cup vegetable oil

*One 16-ounce can whole
tomatoes, chopped, with juice*

*1 tablespoon ghee (p. 93) or
unsalted butter*

*2 tablespoons chopped fresh
coriander, for garnish*

In a large bowl, soak the beans in water to cover at least 8 hours, or overnight; drain.

In a blender, combine the garlic, chilies, and ginger, and process until fine.

Place the beans in a 4-quart pressure cooker. Add the garlic mixture, 6 cups water, the onions, turmeric, ground coriander, ground cumin, chili powder, bay leaves, cumin seeds, asafetida, salt, and oil. Heat to boiling, cover, and cook 20 minutes at 15

Beans and rice for sale at a daily market

pounds pressure, according to manufacturer's instructions. Remove from the heat and reduce the pressure quickly, according to manufacturer's instructions.

Remove the lid and stir in the tomatoes and ghee. Add 1 to 2 cups water if the beans are dry. Heat to boiling, cover, and cook 20 minutes at 15 pounds pressure, or until the beans are soft and the mixture is thickened. Serve garnished with the fresh coriander. Serves 6.

Masoor Dal

S p i c y   R e d   L e n t i l s

Hulled and split red lentils are now available in most supermarkets. Small and pink when dried, they swell and turn yellow when cooked. This method of cooking them with tomatoes gives the dish a rich texture and taste.

1 cup split red lentils (masoor dal), rinsed & picked over

¾ cup finely chopped onions

3 cups water

½ teaspoon ground turmeric

½ teaspoon ground cumin

½ teaspoon ground coriander

½ teaspoon chili powder

2 garlic cloves, halved

1 fresh hot green chili, seeded

One 2-inch piece fresh ginger, peeled & coarsely chopped

1 tablespoon ghee (p. 93) or unsalted butter

One 16-ounce can whole tomatoes, chopped, with juice

3 tablespoons vegetable oil

1½ teaspoons salt

2 tablespoons finely chopped fresh coriander, for garnish

2 medium tomatoes, thinly sliced, for garnish

In a medium saucepan, combine the lentils, onions, water, turmeric, cumin, ground coriander, and chili powder. Heat to boiling, reduce the heat to low, and cook, covered, 30 minutes.

Meanwhile, in a blender, combine the garlic, chili, and ginger, and process until fine. In a small skillet, heat the ghee over medium heat. Add the garlic mixture and cook 2 minutes.

Stir the garlic mixture, chopped tomatoes, oil, and salt into the lentils. Cook, covered, 30 minutes, or until the lentil mixture is thickened. Serve garnished with the fresh coriander and sliced tomatoes. Serves 4 to 6.

Sada Chaval

Plain Buttered Rice *(picture p. 49)*

**Deliciously nutty in flavor, basmati rice is
slightly more expensive than ordinary white rice, but it is fluffy
and aromatic when cooked, and Indians prefer it to any
other kind of rice. Brown basmati has a higher nutritional content than
the white, which is used here, but it's heavier and takes
longer to cook ~ about 40 minutes. Any leftover rice is delicious mixed
with thinly sliced scallions and a beaten egg and fried.**

1 cup basmati rice, well rinsed

1⅔ cups water

½ teaspoon salt

*1 tablespoon ghee (p. 93) or
     unsalted butter*

In a medium bowl, soak the rice 30 minutes in warm water to cover; drain.

In a medium saucepan, combine the rice, water, salt, and ghee. Heat to boiling over high heat. Reduce the heat to low and simmer very gently, covered, 15 minutes, or until the rice is soft and fluffy and all the water has been absorbed. (Do not remove the lid or stir during cooking.) Let sit, covered, 5 minutes. Stir with a fork to fluff. Serves 4 to 6.

Mattar Chaval

Pullao Rice with Peas *(picture p. 39)*

Pullao, from the Persian word "pullo," describes any rice that is cooked with a variety of ingredients. It was introduced to Indian cuisine by the Mughals in the sixteenth century and has since become central to India's culinary repertoire. Pullao rice can be served with almost any Indian dish. For special parties or religious festivals, it is tinted yellow with saffron or turmeric.

1 cup basmati rice, well rinsed

4 tablespoons vegetable oil

½ teaspoon cumin seeds

1¾ cups finely chopped onions

6 cloves

2 cardamom pods, lightly crushed (p. 92)

1 garlic clove, finely chopped

1 cup frozen peas

½ teaspoon salt

In a medium bowl, soak the rice 30 minutes in warm water to cover; drain.

In a medium saucepan, heat 2 tablespoons of the oil over high heat until very hot but not smoking. Add the cumin seeds and cook, stirring constantly, about 5 seconds, or until they pop. Reduce the heat to medium, add half the onions, and cook, stirring frequently, 7 minutes, or until lightly browned. Add the rice, cloves, cardamom, garlic, peas, salt, and water to just cover. Heat to boiling over high heat. Reduce the heat to low and simmer, covered, 15 minutes, or until the rice is soft and fluffy. Let sit, covered, 5 minutes.

Meanwhile, prepare the Garnish: In a medium skillet, heat the remaining oil over high heat. Add the remaining onions and cook 12 minutes, or until well browned.

Serve the hot rice topped with the sizzling onions. Serves 4.

Kesari Chaval

S a f f r o n   R i c e *(picture p. 53)*

This is the special rice dish served at Indian wedding feasts and at Diwali,
the Festival of Lights. The saffron and spices add a delicate flavor and the almonds
provide a pleasant crunch. Tissue-thin pieces of edible gold or silver leaf (vark)
are sometimes used to decorate the rice just before serving.

1 cup basmati rice, well rinsed

Pinch of saffron threads

⅓ cup hot water

1½ tablespoons olive oil

6 garlic cloves, minced

*4 green cardamom pods, cracked
(p. 92)*

One 3-inch cinnamon stick

½ teaspoon salt

½ cup seedless golden raisins

20 whole blanched almonds

2 cups cold water

In a medium bowl, soak the rice 30 minutes in warm water to cover; drain.

In a small bowl, soak the saffron in the hot water 20 minutes.

In a medium saucepan, heat the oil over high heat until very hot but not smoking. Add the garlic, cardamom, and cinnamon, and cook, stirring constantly, 30 seconds, or until the seeds begin to pop. Stir in the rice, salt, raisins, almonds, cold water, and saffron with its soaking liquid. Heat to boiling, reduce the heat to low, and simmer, covered, 15 minutes, or until the rice is light and fluffy. Serves 4.

Sabji ka Chaval

Pullao Rice with Vegetables *(picture p. 45)*

This delicately spiced vegetable dish goes well with most Indian food.
For a change, try substituting golden raisins for the beans and peas. Serve as part
of a vegetarian meal with dal, other vegetable dishes, and Indian bread.

*1½ cups basmati rice, well
  rinsed*

1 tablespoon vegetable oil

¾ cup thinly sliced onions

1 garlic clove, minced

2 large carrots, finely diced

*1 cup haricots verts or
  thin young green beans,
  trimmed & finely diced*

1 cup frozen peas, thawed

*4 green cardamom pods, crushed
  (p. 92)*

6 cloves

One 3-inch cinnamon stick

½ teaspoon salt

2 cups water

*2 tomatoes, quartered, for
  garnish*

In a medium bowl, soak the rice 30 minutes in warm water to cover; drain.

In a medium saucepan, heat the oil over medium-high heat. Add the onions and cook, stirring constantly, 7 minutes, or until lightly browned. Add the garlic and carrots, and cook 3 minutes. Add the rice, beans, peas, cardamom, cloves, cinnamon, salt, and water. Heat to boiling over high heat, reduce the heat to low, and simmer, covered, about 15 minutes, or until the rice is light and fluffy and the vegetables are tender. Serve garnished with the tomatoes. Serves 4 to 6.

Chapatis

Whole-Wheat Flatbread

In India, one of the first tests of a new bride by her
mother-in-law is the quality of her chapatis. A nationwide staple, these
delicate flatbreads are freshly cooked daily on a cast-iron tava, the Indian
version of a griddle, and are served with almost every meal.

*2 cups chapati flour (p. 92) or
1 cup sifted whole-wheat flour
plus 1 cup all-purpose flour*

½ teaspoon salt

About 1 cup water

*Chapati or sifted whole-wheat
flour for dusting*

*Ghee (p. 93) or melted unsalted
butter for serving*

In a large bowl, combine the flour and salt. Slowly stir in just enough water to make a soft dough; it may not be necessary to use a full cup of water. Turn the dough onto a floured surface and knead 8 to 10 minutes, adding more flour if necessary, until the dough is smooth and elastic. (This dough will remain soft and slightly sticky.)

Shape the dough into a ball and place in the bowl. Cover with a clean damp cloth or plastic wrap and set in a warm place at least 30 minutes, or up to 3 hours.

Heat a griddle or skillet to medium heat. Dampen your hands and knead the dough briefly. Divide the dough into 10 portions and shape each portion into a ball. Work with one ball at a time, keeping the remainder covered with a damp towel.

On a lightly floured surface, flatten one ball with the heel of your hand. Dip both sides of the dough in flour and roll it out to a 6-inch round. Rotate it as you roll it out and sprinkle it with flour occasionally to prevent it from sticking.

Slap the chapati back and forth between the palms of your hands to shake off excess flour. Place the chapati on the griddle and cook about one minute, or until the top darkens slightly and small bubbles begin to form. When brownish flecks appear on the underside and the chapati begins to puff up, turn over and cook about 30 seconds. Remove and brush one side with ghee or melted butter. Place in a cloth-lined basket and cover with the cloth to keep warm. Repeat the process until all the chapatis are cooked. Makes 8 to 10.

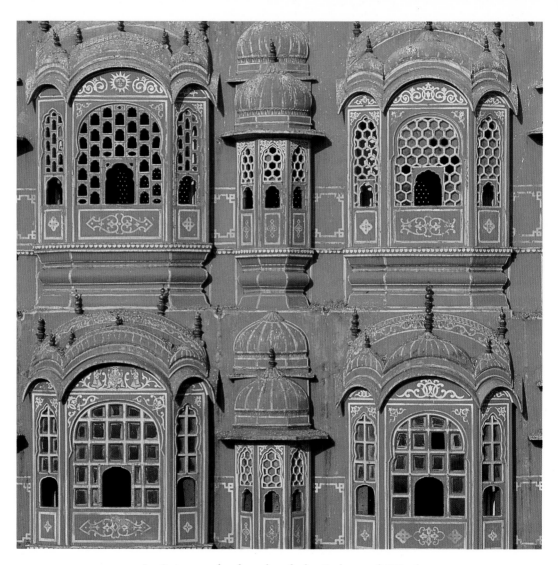

In Jaipur, the facade of the Palace of Wind

Paratha

**Wheat is the staple grain in most Indian diets, and Indians make
a variety of breads from whole-wheat and lighter flours. Parathas, slightly
richer than Chapatis (p. 82), are equally universal.**

*Prepared dough for Chapatis
(p. 82)*

*6 tablespoons melted ghee (p. 93)
or 3 tablespoons melted
unsalted butter blended with
3 tablespoons vegetable oil*

Heat a griddle or skillet to medium heat. Divide the dough into 6 portions and shape each portion into a ball. Work with one ball at a time, keeping the remainder covered with a damp towel.

On a lightly floured surface, roll out one dough ball into a 9-inch round. Brush the top with 1 teaspoon of the ghee. Fold the dough over to form a half circle and brush the top with ½ teaspoon ghee. Fold in half again and tuck under any uneven edges. Roll out again to a 9-inch round and brush the top with ½ teaspoon ghee.

Brush the hot griddle with ½ teaspoon ghee. Place the paratha on the griddle and cook, rotating the bread every 5 to 7 seconds, about 1½ minutes per side, or until lightly browned; watch carefully so the paratha does not burn. If necessary, brush the griddle again with ½ teaspoon ghee to prevent the paratha from sticking. Remove the paratha with a spatula and place on a large cloth-lined plate; cover with the cloth while making the remaining parathas. Makes 6 large parathas.

Aloo Paratha

Potato-Stuffed Flatbread *(picture p. 88)*

**Stuffed parathas are served as
a satisfying snack or small meal with chutney or salted yogurt.**

Filling:

*1 tablespoon ghee (p. 93) or
  unsalted butter*

½ teaspoon chili powder

*½ teaspoon pomegranate seeds
  (p. 94), crushed (optional)*

*½ teaspoon garam masala
  (p. 93)*

*1 medium fresh hot green chili,
  seeded & minced*

*2 cups coarsely mashed
  cooked potatoes*

*Prepared dough for Chapatis
  (p. 82)*

*¼ cup melted ghee (p. 93) or
  2 tablespoons melted
  unsalted butter blended with
  2 tablespoons vegetable oil*

Prepare the Filling: In a small saucepan, heat the ghee over high heat until very hot but not smoking. Add the chili powder, pomegranate seeds if desired, garam masala, and chili, and cook, stirring constantly, 30 seconds. Transfer to a medium bowl, add the potatoes, and stir until well blended. Set aside.

Heat a griddle or skillet to medium heat. Divide the dough into 6 portions and shape each portion into a ball. Work with one ball at a time, keeping the remainder covered with a clean damp towel.

On a lightly floured surface, roll one dough ball into a 9-inch round. Spread one-sixth of the filling over half of the paratha, spreading it to ¼ inch from the edge. Fold the other half of the paratha over the filling to form a half circle and pinch the edges to seal. Brush the top with ½ teaspoon of the melted ghee.

Sweet milk tea is enjoyed in the morning throughout India

Fold in half again and tuck under any uneven edges. Roll out again to a 9-inch round. Brush the top with ½ teaspoon ghee.

Brush the griddle with 1 teaspoon ghee. Place the paratha on the griddle and cook, rotating every 5 to 7 seconds, 1½ to 2 minutes per side, or until lightly browned. If necessary, brush the griddle again with ½ teaspoon ghee. Remove the paratha with a spatula. Set aside on a large cloth-lined plate; cover with the cloth while making the remaining parathas. Makes 6 large parathas.

Keema Parathas & Aloo Parathas, page 86

Keema Paratha

Meat-Stuffed Flatbread

**These stuffed parathas are often served at breakfast
with fried eggs and hot tea, or as a snack with sweetened or spiced yogurt.**

*Prepared dough for Chapatis
(p. 82)*

*1 recipe Shami Kebab mixture
(p. 22), omitting split peas*

*¼ cup melted ghee (p. 93) or
2 tablespoons melted
unsalted butter blended with
2 tablespoons vegetable oil*

Heat a griddle or skillet over medium heat. Divide the dough into 6 portions and shape each portion into a ball. Work with one ball at a time, keeping the remainder covered with a damp towel.

On a lightly floured surface, roll one ball into a 9-inch round. Spread one-sixth of the shami kebab filling over half of the paratha, spreading it to ¼ inch from the edge. Fold the other half of the paratha over the filling to form a half circle and pinch the edges to seal. Brush the top with ½ teaspoon ghee. Fold the

paratha in half again and tuck any uneven edges under. Roll out again to a 9-inch round. Brush the top with ½ teaspoon melted ghee.

Brush the grill with 1 teaspoon ghee. Place the paratha on the griddle and cook, rotating every 5 to 7 seconds, 1½ minutes per side, or until lightly browned. If necessary, brush the griddle again with ½ teaspoon ghee. Remove the paratha with a spatula to a large cloth-lined plate; cover with the cloth while you make the remaining parathas. Makes 6 large parathas.

Poori

Fried Puffed Whole-Wheat Bread

These feather-light little breads puff when
they are fried, for a heavenly look and a rich taste that makes them
great for entertaining. With a little practice, you can roll out
the pastry and fry the breads one after another at an even pace. Beginners
may find it easier to roll out a quantity of pooris, then fry
them in batches. They should be eaten hot, for they deflate as they
cool and they can't be reheated.

Prepared dough for Chapatis
(p. 82)

2 cups vegetable oil

Divide the dough into 25 portions and shape each portion into a ball. On a lightly floured surface, roll out each ball of dough to a 4-inch round.

In a large deep skillet, heat the oil over medium heat to 365°F.

Using a slotted spoon, place the pooris, four at a time, in the oil. With the spoon, hold the pooris under the oil or gently swish oil over the surface of the breads with the spoon until the pooris balloon up and turn light brown, 15 to 20 seconds.

Turn the pooris over and cook 10 to 15 seconds. Drain on paper towels and keep warm in a 275°F oven while you fry the remaining pooris. Stacked slightly overlapping on paper towels, the breads will remain puffy about 30 minutes in the oven. Makes 25 pooris.

Most Indian dishes can be prepared with these spices and ingredients. They can be found at Indian groceries and many gourmet specialty stores.

STORING AND USING SPICES

All spices lose their essential oils and flavors in storage, so it is always best to buy them in small quantities and replace them regularly. Keep them in airtight containers away from the light, and label and date them to ensure a turnover every three months. Most spices are available in ground form, but it is far better to buy them whole and then dry-roast and grind them at home when you need them.

TO DRY-ROAST SPICES: Heat a heavy pan over medium-low heat, 3 to 4 minutes. Add the harder spices first (for example, fenugreek or cinnamon before coriander or cumin) and cook them, stirring, until they take on color and give off a pleasant aroma, about 3 to 4 minutes. Take care that they do not blacken and burn, or they will become bitter. Remove them from the pan and allow to cool before grinding them or using whole.

Ajowan: This poppy-seed like spice comes from the lovage plant and is sometimes sold under its botanical name, *Carom*. It has a strong peppery thyme flavor, and it is popular in northern Indian cooking. It is used sparingly and is especially good with potatoes and other root vegetables. Thyme is a suitable substitute.

Asafetida *(hing)*: This is a strong-tasting spice, with a pronounced garlic flavor. It is used in small quantities to aid digestion and prevent flatulence ~ particularly when lentils and other beans are served.

Basmati rice: This fragrant, long-grained rice, grown in India and Pakistan, is the preferred rice for Indian cooking.

Cardamom *(elaichi)*: Essential to Indian cooking, this spice is available in whole green pods *(choti elaichi)*, black pods *(badi elaichi)*, and ground.

Green cardamom is known as one of the "warm spices" and is an essential ingredient of garam masala. It has a pungent, highly aromatic, eucalyptus like flavor. Its pale green seed pods contain sticky black or dark brown seeds; the seeds are also sold ready-ground. Green cardamom is often chewed after meals to aid in digestion.

Black cardamom is coarser in flavor and larger in size. It is used in meat, poultry, and rice dishes; it cannot be eaten raw.

When whole or cracked pods are used in Indian recipes, they flavor the dish but are not usually meant to be eaten. Be sure to use pods when called for; ground cardamom is not a good substitute in such recipes.

Chapati flour *(atta)*: This very finely ground low-gluten whole-wheat flour is used for making chapatis and other Indian flatbreads. If chapati flour is unavailable, substitute 2 parts sifted whole-wheat flour mixed with 2 parts unbleached all-purpose flour.

Chick pea flour: Besan or gram flour is a fine, pale-yellow flour made from ground chick peas (garbanzos). It is used for making pakoras and other fried snacks and savories.

Chili pepper: The hot green chili peppers used in so much Indian cooking are the pods of the plant *Capsicum*. The widely available bright green jalapeño and serrano peppers range from hot to very hot and are a good choice for most Indian recipes. Choose fresh green peppers 1 to 2 inches in length with no soft or brown spots. Handle carefully, as the heat resides in the seeds and the oil they give off is an irritant that can remain on your hands.

Cumin *(jeera)*: This aromatic, pungent spice is widely used both as whole seeds or ground. A relative of caraway, whole cumin is available in two varieties: black and white. Most ready-ground cumin is from the white seed, which is much less expensive than the black. Black cumin is treasured for its intense and complex flavor. White cumin, however, is a fine substitute. To bring out the flavor of this spice, dry-roast or fry briefly in very hot oil.

Dal: The general term in India for all types of dried beans, peas, and lentils, which are available whole or split. Dal comes in many varieties, including yellow split peas *(chana dal)*, mung beans *(mung dal)*, Egyptian red lentils *(masoor dal)*, red kidney beans *(rajma)*, pigeon peas *(toovar dal)*, and dried black lentils *(urad dal)*. A valuable source of protein, especially for vegetarians, dal is easy to cook ~ especially in a pressure cooker ~ and easy to digest, given the addition of asafetida. Dal is included in most meals all over the subcontinent.

Fenugreek *(methi)*: Available fresh in summer, fenugreek leaves are used in meat dishes, potatoes, and in breads. Dried fenugreek has a very pungent, bitter taste and should be used sparingly. The dried yellow-brown seeds are used whole or ground. Spinach is a good substitute for fresh fenugreek.

Garam Masala: An essential spice mixture in Indian cooking; its name means "warm spices." This is an aromatic mix that is sprinkled on just as a dish is finished. It is sold commercially or can be made at home. Grind together in a spice mill or mortar with pestle 1 tablespoon black peppercorns, 2 teaspoons cumin seeds, one 1-inch piece cinnamon stick, 10 green cardamom pods, 1 teaspoon cloves, and 3 bay leaves. Store in an airtight container. Makes about 3 tablespoons.

Ghee: This is a clarified butter used extensively in Indian cooking. Unlike ordinary butter, it can be used for frying at a very high heat. It is sold in cans as pure butter ghee or, less expensively, as ghee-with-vegetable oil. Ghee can seem rather heavy and rich, so it's best to add very small amounts to food just before serving to produce a distinctive flavor. Once opened, it will keep in the refrigerator in a well-sealed container for up to 6 months.

Jaggery: An unrefined sugar with a unique musky flavor, jaggery is made from the juice of sugar-cane stalks. It is usually packaged in large lumps. Dark brown sugar can be used as a substitute.

Kalonji: These small jet-black seeds, also called *nigella,* or black onion seeds, have a distinctive peppery taste. Use in dals, vegetable dishes, pickles, and stuffed breads.

Mango, dried *(amchoor)*: A spice powder made from sun-dried unripe mangoes, this adds sourness to a dish in the same way as tamarind, pomegranate seeds, and lemon juice do.

Mustard seeds, whole black *(rai)*: These small brownish-black spicy seeds are especially popular in the cooking of eastern and southern India. They are often used in fish dishes and as a flavoring for chutneys. Fried whole in hot oil as the first step of a recipe, they impart a sweet and earthy flavor. If ground, their flavor is pungent and bitter.

Pomegranate seeds *(anardana)*: The sun-dried kernels of the wild pomegranate are used to add a tang and crunch to vegetables, meat dishes, and dals, especially in the cooking of northwestern India. Mango powder sometimes can be substituted for flavor, but nothing can substitute for the texture the seeds add to a dish.

Saffron *(zaafraan)*: The most expensive spice in the world is made from the dried stamens of crocuses. Highly aromatic, it also lends a delicate yellow color to rice dishes. Don't use too much saffron, or it will add a bitter taste.

Shahi Masala: A zesty combination of several piquant spices, this mixture is used in marinades and braised meat dishes. In a blender or spice grinder, combine seeds from 12 black cardamom pods, seeds from 10 green cardamom pods, 1½ teaspoons black peppercorns, 1 teaspoon ground turmeric, 1 teaspoon ground cumin, 1 teaspoon ground coriander, 1 teaspoon chili powder, 1 teaspoon fenugreek seeds, 1 teaspoon fennel seeds, a pinch of ajowan, and a pinch of asafetida. Process until fine. Store in a small jar with a tight-fitting lid. Makes 6 tablespoons.

Tamarind *(imli)*: These large bean pods have a distinctive sour taste. They are seeded and pressed into semidried pulp, from which the juice is extracted. The juice adds a sweet-and-sour flavor to certain dishes, most often fish and seafood.

Tamarind is available in pulp form, which must be soaked and strained, or as tamarind concentrate, which needs no soaking. The soaked and strained pulp will not keep for long, so make it up as you need it. Tamarind concentrate, once opened, keeps refrigerated up to 3 months.

Tandoori Masala: This mixture is used to flavor and add a distinctive red color to poultry and meat dishes. In a small bowl, combine 2 tablespoons shahi masala, 1 teaspoon ground turmeric, 1 teaspoon ground coriander, 1 teaspoon red food coloring powder, and a pinch of asafetida. Store in a small jar with a tight-fitting lid. Makes about 3 tablespoons.

Turmeric *(haldi)*: Usually sold ground, turmeric comes from the dried rhizome of a plant in the ginger family. A strong yellow spice, it is used sparingly in many Indian dishes to add color and flavor.

WEIGHTS

Ounces and Pounds	Metrics
¼ ounce	7 grams
⅓ ounce	10 grams
½ ounce	14 grams
1 ounce	28 grams
1½ ounces	42 grams
1¾ ounces	50 grams
2 ounces	57 grams
3 ounces	85 grams
3½ ounces	100 grams
4 ounces (¼ pound)	114 grams
6 ounces	170 grams
8 ounces (½ pound)	227 grams
9 ounces	250 grams
16 ounces (1 pound)	464 grams

LIQUID MEASURES

tsp.: teaspoon
Tbs.: tablespoon

Spoons and Cups	Metric Equivalents
¼ tsp.	1.23 milliliters
½ tsp.	2.5 milliliters
¾ tsp.	3.7 milliliters
1 tsp.	5 milliliters
1 dessertspoon	10 milliliters
1 Tbs. (3 tsp.)	15 milliliters
2 Tbs. (1 ounce)	30 milliliters
¼ cup	60 milliliters
⅓ cup	80 milliliters
½ cup	120 milliliters
⅔ cup	160 milliliters
¾ cup	180 milliliters
1 cup (8 ounces)	240 milliliters
2 cups (1 pint)	480 milliliters
3 cups	720 milliliters
4 cups (1 quart)	1 litre
4 quarts (1 gallon)	3¾ litres

TEMPERATURES

°F (Fahrenheit)	°C (Centigrade or Celsius)
32 (water freezes)	0
200	95
212 (water boils)	100
250	120
275	135
300 (slow oven)	150
325	160
350 (moderate oven)	175
375	190
400 (hot oven)	205
425	220
450 (very hot oven)	232
475	245
500 (extremely hot oven)	260

LENGTH

U.S. Measurements	Metric Equivalents
⅛ inch	3mm
¼ inch	6mm
⅜ inch	1 cm
½ inch	1.2 cm
¾ inch	2 cm
1 inch	2.5 cm
1¼ inches	3.1 cm
1½ inches	3.7 cm
2 inches	5 cm
3 inches	7.5 cm
4 inches	10 cm
5 inches	12.5 cm

APPROXIMATE EQUIVALENTS

1 kilo is slightly more than 2 pounds
1 litre is slightly more than 1 quart
1 meter is slightly over 3 feet
1 centimeter is approximately ⅜ inch

INDEX